She Persisted

RUBY BRIDGES

―INSPIRED BY―
She Persisted
by Chelsea Clinton & Alexandra Boiger

....

RUBY BRIDGES

....

Written by
Kekla Magoon

Interior illustrations by
Gillian Flint

PHILOMEL

PHILOMEL BOOKS
An imprint of Penguin Random House LLC, New York

First published in the United States of America by Philomel,
an imprint of Penguin Random House LLC, 2021.

Text copyright © 2021 by Chelsea Clinton.
Illustrations copyright © 2021 by Alexandra Boiger.

Penguin supports copyright. Copyright fuels creativity, encourages diverse
voices, promotes free speech, and creates a vibrant culture. Thank you for
buying an authorized edition of this book and for complying with copyright
laws by not reproducing, scanning, or distributing any part of it in any
form without permission. You are supporting writers and allowing Penguin
to continue to publish books for every reader.

Philomel Books is a registered trademark of Penguin Random House LLC.

Visit us online at penguinrandomhouse.com.

Library of Congress Cataloging-in-Publication Data is available.

Printed in Italy

HC ISBN 9780593115862
PB ISBN 9780593115879

10 9 8 7 6 5 4 3 2 1
GFV

Edited by Jill Santopolo.
Design by Ellice M. Lee.
Text set in LTC Kennerley.

The publisher does not have any control over and does not assume any
responsibility for author or third-party websites or their content.

For
Lia and Iris

She Persisted

....

She Persisted: HARRIET TUBMAN

She Persisted: CLAUDETTE COLVIN

She Persisted: SALLY RIDE

She Persisted: VIRGINIA APGAR

She Persisted: NELLIE BLY

She Persisted: SONIA SOTOMAYOR

She Persisted: FLORENCE GRIFFITH JOYNER

She Persisted: RUBY BRIDGES

She Persisted: CLARA LEMLICH

She Persisted: MARGARET CHASE SMITH

She Persisted: MARIA TALLCHIEF

She Persisted: HELEN KELLER

She Persisted: OPRAH WINFREY

Dear Reader,

As Sally Ride and Marian Wright Edelman both powerfully said, "You can't be what you can't see." When Sally Ride said that, she meant that it was hard to dream of being an astronaut, like she was, or a doctor or an athlete or anything at all if you didn't see someone like you who already had lived that dream. She especially was talking about seeing women in jobs that historically were held by men.

I wrote the first *She Persisted* and the books that came after it because I wanted young girls—and children of all genders—to see women who worked hard to live their dreams. And I wanted all of us to see examples of persistence in the face of different challenges to help inspire us in our own lives.

I'm so thrilled now to partner with a sisterhood of writers to bring longer, more in-depth versions of these stories of women's persistence and achievement to readers. I hope you enjoy these chapter books as much as I do and find them inspiring and empowering.

And remember: If anyone ever tells you no, if anyone ever says your voice isn't important or your dreams are too big, remember these women. They persisted and so should you.

Warmly,
Chelsea Clinton

RUBY BRIDGES

TABLE OF CONTENTS

Chapter 1: *From the Family Farm to the Big City* . . 1

Chapter 2: *An Important Test* 9

Chapter 3: *The First Day of School* 15

Chapter 4: *A Classroom for One* 22

Chapter 5: *Following Ruby's Lead* 30

Chapter 6: *The Power of Children* 36

How You Can Persist 42

References 48

CHAPTER I
....

From the Family Farm to the Big City

When Ruby Bridges was born in 1954, her parents brought her home, full of hope that their daughter would grow up in a better world than they had. Little did they know how big a role Ruby herself would play in building that better world.

Ruby and her parents lived on her grandparents' farm in Tylertown, Mississippi. The family loved their land, and they loved being together.

Farming was very challenging work. Everyone helped out, even young Ruby! As she grew, she visited her other grandparents' farm, too. She and her cousins picked beans and cucumbers and helped with canning to preserve them.

The Bridges family worked very hard, but they did not have a lot of money. Ruby's father tried to get another job to help support the family, but it was hard to find a business that would hire him.

The United States of America was a difficult place for Black people, like Ruby's family, to live. Mississippi was an especially hard place for a Black family to live, because of certain laws that affected Black people. These laws enforced a system called segregation. Segregation laws kept Black people and white people apart. They had to eat in separate restaurants and live in separate neighborhoods. At movie theaters, there was one door for white people and a separate door for Black people. On every bus, there were separate seating sections for Black people and white people. In the park, there was one drinking fountain for Black people and another one for white people. Black children went to all-Black schools and white children went to all-white schools.

The worst part was the schools, water fountains, and seating areas for Black people were not as nice as the ones for white people. This was very unfair. Black people felt angry and frustrated about the way they were being treated. But the country had been using segregation laws for a long time, and people were used to it. Some people were eager to see these laws change, but many others were afraid.

When Ruby was two or three years old, running around on her grandparents' farm, she had no idea what segregation was. She did not know that people were going to treat her unfairly because of the color of her skin. She had never even spoken to a white person! She was happy in her all-Black world.

Ruby's parents knew all about segregation. They worried about Ruby's future. Ruby's parents did not know how to read or write, because they hadn't been able to go to school. They wanted Ruby to have a chance to learn. They wanted her to have every opportunity that a white child might have. So they decided to leave their small Mississippi town and move to New Orleans, Louisiana. Ruby's parents believed that living in a big city would give Ruby a chance to go to a good school.

Why? Well, in 1954, the year Ruby was born, something important had happened. The United States Supreme Court, the highest court in the land, heard a story about a Black girl named Linda Brown who wanted to go to the best school in her city, which was an all-white school. After hearing her story, the Supreme Court decided that segregation laws were unfair because they stopped Black children like Linda from going to the best schools. The court ordered schools across the country to integrate, which meant that they needed to allow Black and white students to attend the same schools.

Ruby was four years old when her family moved to New Orleans. It had also been four years since the Supreme Court ordered schools to integrate, but New Orleans schools were still segregated.

Ruby had not started school yet, but she knew that she would start kindergarten soon. Her family moved into two bedrooms of a house in an all-Black neighborhood. Ruby and her three younger siblings shared a bedroom. She missed her

grandparents and the farm, but she was able to visit them in the summer. "My world in those days was comfortable and safe," Ruby said.

She did not know that was about to change.

CHAPTER 2
....

An Important Test

Ruby did get to go to school in New Orleans, just like her parents had hoped. When she was five years old, she started kindergarten at Johnson Lockett Elementary School. It was an all-Black school. Even though the Supreme Court had ordered schools to integrate, Louisiana was one of several states that were very slow to change.

Ruby loved kindergarten. She was good at

school. She got high grades, she behaved well in class and she made new friends.

Toward the end of the school year, Ruby's mother told her that she was going to be taking a special test. One day, she and her mother got dressed up and went downtown. They rode the bus to the school board building. They went inside, where they were sent to wait in a huge room. It was full of about a hundred other Black children. They were all going to be taking the same test.

Ruby took the test, but she didn't have any idea why she was taking it. The truth was New Orleans schools were finally going to be integrated. The test would help decide which Black students would go to all-white schools.

The test was very hard, on purpose. The white people who designed the test hoped it would be so hard that none of the Black students would pass. But Ruby did pass. She was one of only six students who did! And so that summer, Ruby was invited to attend William Frantz Elementary School, an all-white school.

There were several good things about William Frantz Elementary School. It was very close to Ruby's house, much closer than her old school had been. It was also known to be a very good school, better than her old school had been. And it would be the first time that a Black student had gone to William Frantz, so Ruby would be part of a much bigger change taking place across the country—a change known as the civil rights movement.

Ruby's parents weren't sure that sending their daughter to William Frantz was a good idea. A lot of people were very angry about the idea of integration. Sending Ruby to an all-white school might put their whole family in danger.

At first, Ruby's father said "No!" He did not want to put Ruby, or the rest of them, at risk. But Ruby's mother knew it was the right thing to do. They discussed, debated and argued. Important people came to their house to talk to Ruby's parents. Lawyers and activists from an organization called the National Association for the Advancement of Colored People (NAACP) reminded Ruby's parents that this opportunity was a very big deal. The NAACP lawyers and activists had worked hard to get the courts to support integration in the first place, so their opinion mattered a lot to Ruby's family.

Ruby's parents did not stop feeling afraid, but they believed strongly in their daughter's education. They decided to be brave. Finally, Ruby's parents agreed to let her go to the new school.

"I was going to integrate William Frantz

public school, and I was going alone," Ruby said. For Ruby herself, there was never really a choice. She simply followed her parents' instructions. "If they told you to do something, you did it," she said.

The night before Ruby's first day at the new school, her mother tried hard to prepare her for the strange things ahead. "There might be a lot of people outside the school," Ruby's mother told her. "But you don't need to be afraid."

At that moment, Ruby was not afraid. She was only sad that she was not going to be in the same school with her friends anymore. At six years old, she had no idea what a huge moment in history she was about to be a part of.

CHAPTER 3

The First Day of School

At William Frantz, the school year started in September. That year, 1960, Ruby did not start school there in September like the other children. She had to wait, because people who did not want school integration to happen were trying to get the courts to change their mind. It was mid-November before Ruby started attending her new school.

On Ruby's first day of school, several large

men came to the Bridges family's front door. The men were federal marshals, which meant they were like police officers who worked for the U.S. government. They offered Ruby a ride to school in their car. This was a bit strange. After all, the William Frantz school was only a few blocks from Ruby's house. Most students walked to school.

"I learned later they were carrying guns," Ruby explained about the marshals. Many white people in New Orleans were angry that the schools were being integrated. The U.S. government feared that some of the angry people might try to hurt Ruby, so the marshals were there to protect her.

Ruby acted very bravely that day. She got into the car with the federal marshals and her mother, who made Ruby promise to behave herself at school. They drove the few blocks. The drive took longer than usual, because there were hundreds of people blocking the street.

When Ruby first saw the crowd, she thought maybe they were there for Mardi Gras. Mardi Gras is a huge carnival celebration that takes place every spring in New Orleans—except it was November, which was not the right time of year for Mardi

Gras. But the crowd had that kind of excited energy about it. People were laughing and smiling even though they were there for a very upsetting purpose: to prevent one small girl from going to school. The white protestors began to chant: "Two, four, six, eight, we don't want to integrate!"

The marshals got out of the car first, and Ruby came out after them. She couldn't see the faces of anyone in the crowd. She was small, and the marshals stood protectively around her, blocking her view. They walked through the crowd, toward the school. When they got closer, Ruby could see that the school building looked bigger and fancier than her previous school. It seemed like an important place.

Ruby and her mother went to the principal's office and waited there. They waited and waited.

"We didn't talk to anybody," Ruby recalled. "I remember watching a big round clock on the wall. When it was 3:00 and time to go home, I was glad." On that first day at William Frantz Elementary

School, Ruby didn't even set foot in a classroom!

Meanwhile, there was a great deal of chaos going on in the school. White parents raced into the office and into the classrooms, pulling their children out of the building in protest. The crowd outside grew larger. Many white people remained angry, and confused about why their protest hadn't worked.

When Ruby and her mother walked out of school, the crowd had grown even bigger. Protestors held signs with threatening messages. They shouted hateful words at Ruby. One protestor had a Black doll in a coffin. It was a threat. When Ruby noticed that doll on her way out of school, it was the scariest thing she had ever seen. That moment was perhaps the first time she realized that she and her family were risking their lives to help make integrated schools a reality in New Orleans.

That night, Ruby's father called her his brave little girl. She had been brave indeed, and she would have to keep being brave. The hardest part of her journey was still to come.

CHAPTER 4
....

A Classroom for One

On Ruby's second day at William Frantz, there was still a big crowd outside the school. There was still a lot of anger and shouting. But inside, it was safe.

Ruby went to her first-grade classroom. She met her teacher, a white woman named Mrs. Barbara Henry. At first, Ruby was surprised to be the only student in Mrs. Henry's class. The school had decided to move all the white children to a different classroom. The school had to allow Black students into the building, but some teachers hoped they could still keep classes segregated.

Every day after that, Ruby and Mrs. Henry spent all day alone in the classroom, with the federal marshals guarding the door outside. "I grew to love Ruby and to be awed by her," Mrs. Henry said. "It was an ugly world outside, but I tried to make our world together as normal as possible."

Mrs. Henry and Ruby sat side by side in the classroom doing lessons. Sometimes they would go together to the chalkboard and work there instead. They practiced reading and spelling and math. They sang songs, did puzzles and played games to fill the time.

Ruby was not allowed to go to the cafeteria or the playground. She had to spend her lunch

hour all alone in the classroom, while Mrs. Henry had her lunch with the other teachers. Some days, Ruby did not eat the sandwich her mother had packed. She hid it instead, hoping that she might get invited to join the others in the cafeteria. When Mrs. Henry found out, she began staying with Ruby to keep her company during lunchtime, too. "I became very attached to her," Ruby said. "She had a polite, kind manner that I admired."

Mrs. Henry and Ruby liked each other very much, but it was often hard to have school with just two people. Mrs. Henry missed teaching a full class of students. Ruby missed having other children to talk to. It was a difficult time for both of them. Still, "neither one of us ever missed a day," Mrs. Henry said later on. "It was important to keep going."

Ruby's world consisted of school with Mrs. Henry during the day, spending time with her friends in her Black community in the afternoons and being home with her parents and siblings in the evenings. At first, it was hard for her to imagine all the unrest that was happening around New Orleans during that time, all because one little Black girl was going to a new school. White people were still angrily protesting.

Ruby's family's choice to support integration began to affect the family more and more. They received threatening notes. White-owned stores turned Ruby's mother away. Ruby's father was fired from his job. Neighbors guarded their house at night, to make sure no one came to act on the terrible threats.

People around the country knew that Ruby's

family was going through a hard time. Many people wrote letters to encourage Ruby, and to remind her whole family to stay strong. Some people even sent money to help them survive while Ruby's father struggled to find a new job. Many people appreciated what Ruby was doing.

Going to school every day might have seemed like a normal thing to do, but for Ruby it was so much more. As the first Black student at William Frantz Elementary School, Ruby was setting a great example of what equal education could be like.

When the school year was almost over, Mrs. Henry convinced the other teachers to let the white students from the other first-grade class spend time with Ruby. There were only four students in that class, because so many parents were keeping their children out of school in protest. One of the white boys refused to play with her because she was Black. Finally, Ruby understood why she had been kept apart from the others.

At the end of the school year, Mrs. Henry gave Ruby very high grades in all her subjects. She had learned so much! But the principal tried to lower Ruby's grades. Some people still did not want Ruby's hard work to prove that Black and white students could learn together in the same school, and that they could all do well.

But a big change was coming. One principal could not stop it. Not even the big angry crowd of hundreds could stop it. Soon, more schools in New Orleans and all around the country would follow Ruby's example. It sounds amazing, but one six-year-old girl helped all Black people across the whole country gain the chance for an equal education.

CHAPTER 5
....

Following Ruby's Lead

When Ruby returned to William Frantz Elementary School for second grade, everything was different. There were many other children in her class! That was exciting. Most of the children were white, but a few of them were Black. Integration was finally happening as it was meant to.

The teacher at the front of the room was different, too. Mrs. Henry was nowhere to be found.

Not in Ruby's classroom, and not anywhere in all of William Frantz school! Ruby was heartbroken. She loved Mrs. Henry, and she had expected to see her in second grade. But Mrs. Henry had moved back to Boston, Massachusetts, her hometown. Ruby would not see her again for many years.

Ruby's second-grade year was much more normal than her first-grade year had been. She made friends, she worked hard in class and she followed her teacher's instructions. She did not think this new teacher liked her very much, though. She said unkind things to Ruby and sometimes made her feel sad. Ruby felt different from her classmates, and not just because of her skin color. Sometimes people teased her, even the teacher. But Ruby kept learning and growing all the same.

As Ruby got older, she began to understand

how important her first-grade year had been. While it was happening, she had not realized that the whole country was watching her go to school every day! Her picture had appeared in newspapers and magazines. A famous artist named Norman Rockwell had even painted a picture of her walking into William Frantz, escorted by the federal marshals. The painting became very famous. Ruby saw a copy of it for the first time when she was seventeen, about to graduate from high school. The original hangs in a museum, where Ruby would finally see it in person many years later.

It amazed Ruby to recognize that she had made an important contribution to American history. It felt strange, but good. She began to wonder if there were other ways she could make a difference now that she was older.

When Ruby graduated from high school, she became a travel agent. Her job involved helping people plan trips, buy train tickets and airplane tickets and make hotel reservations. Ruby met a man named Malcolm Hall, and they got married in 1984. Ruby was thirty years old.

Soon, Ruby had children of her own, and she wondered about their futures just like her parents had wondered about hers.

"Young children never know about racism at the start," Ruby said. They start out knowing the truth—that all people, regardless of skin color, are the same on the inside. Racism, which is the idea that people with different skin colors should be treated differently, was invented by adults. It had to be taught.

Ruby knew that if she talked to children about her experiences, they could understand how bad it had felt to be treated unfairly because of her skin color. Once other children heard her story, they might not believe the grown-ups who tried to talk about differences between people of different races. Children, Ruby knew, could be leaders. Children had the power to affect the way the whole country thought about race.

CHAPTER 6
....

The Power of Children

When she was forty-five years old, Ruby created a charity organization called the Ruby Bridges Foundation. Her plan was to raise money for programs to help children learn about overcoming racism. Through her foundation, Ruby worked with young people in schools and communities across the country. "I chose integration as my life's work," she said.

Ruby believed in telling the truth about

American history to children, and she began by telling her own truth. Then she told about other difficult times in the past when Black people were treated unfairly, and she told them that people of all races needed to work together to make sure that everyone would be treated fairly in the future. She said, "If our children are to learn from our history, then we must teach it." And she did.

In 2000, Ruby was named an honorary deputy federal marshal. The marshals were still grateful for and impressed by the courage Ruby had shown years before as a first grader. Ruby went to Washington, DC, for a ceremony. She was so proud to be honored by the people who had protected her. "Deputy U.S. marshals are peacemakers and advocates of justice," Ruby said. She worked hard to be those things too.

When Ruby met President Barack Obama, the first Black president of the United States, he thanked her for what she had done as a six-year-old. President Obama said, "If it hadn't been for you . . .

I might not be here." He meant that without Ruby, and without everyone who worked hard for equal rights like she did, the United States might not have been ready to elect a Black president in 2008, less than fifty years after Ruby's first day of school at William Frantz.

For Ruby, it was strange and sad to think about all the mistakes her country had made in the past. Some of those mistakes were still being made, but it felt good to be on the path of correcting them, and helping to make sure things got better in the future. It felt good to be standing in a world where children of all colors and backgrounds could learn together in the same classrooms. It felt good to be working hard to make a difference in the lives of children of a whole new generation.

"There's more work that I need to do, and I

would hope that everyone else feels the same way," Ruby said. "If we are to get past our racial differences, it is going to come from our kids."

In 2014, a statue of six-year-old Ruby Bridges went up in front of William Frantz Elementary School. Ruby's statue and her story are always there to remind people that you don't have to be a big person to make a big difference in the world.

When she was just six years old, Ruby Bridges was a trailblazer. She went to school all alone every day, and she never gave up on the idea of integration. As an adult, Ruby never gave up either. Today, she makes a difference by sharing her truth. She continues to spend her life helping others blaze new trails—of education, of opportunity, of equality. Ruby Bridges persisted—and you can too.

HOW YOU CAN PERSIST

by Kekla Magoon

If you want to help your community get past racial differences, and stand up for equality like Ruby did, here are some ideas:

1. Spend time with people who look very different than you do.
2. If you hear someone say something unkind to a person of a different race, or repeat a stereotype about a group of

people, speak up and remind them that people of all backgrounds are equal and important.
3. Make a sign that says, "All people are equal," and put it in your window. You could also carry it to a local civil rights demonstration.
4. Write a letter to an elected official expressing your support for laws that promote equality.
5. Do a school project about the civil rights movement and share it with your friends and classmates.
6. Ask your local library and your school library to buy books that help people learn about the civil rights movement.
7. Read a book written by a Black author.

Then read another.

8. Encourage the grown-ups in your life to vote for candidates who support equality. Ask an adult to take you with them to the polls on election day so you can observe democracy in action.

9. Share Ruby's story with your friends and family, to help them understand the important history of school integration.

Acknowledgments

Every book takes a village, and I feel constant gratitude for the many people who support me in the writing process. Thanks to Will, Alice, Lia, and Iris for offering me a home away from home; to Cynthia, Emily, Kerry, Nicole, and Sarah for many moments of shared laughter and ever-important writerly guidance; to my colleagues in the Vermont College of Fine Arts faculty and alumnx communities; and to my agent, Ginger Knowlton. Thanks to my editors, Jill Santopolo and Talia Benamy, for their enthusiasm and thoughtful suggestions, as well as everyone at Philomel who worked so hard to take this book from an idea to a reality. And a special thanks to Chelsea Clinton for inviting me to participate in this series!

References

"Activist Ruby Bridges on Racism in America Today." PBS. May 3, 2018. https://www.pbs.org/video/activist-ruby-bridges-racism-america-today-2g2lfs/.

Bridges, Ruby. *Through My Eyes*. New York: Scholastic, 1999.

———. "We Are All Going Against the Grain."

TEDxNapaValley. April 29, 2014. https://youtu.be/lyRH_LK8v5c.

Byrd-McDevitt, Lori. "10 Facts About Ruby Bridges." The Children's Museum of Indianapolis. November 15, 2016. https://www.childrensmuseum.org/blog/10-facts-about-ruby-bridges.

"Freedom's Legacy: A Conversation with Ruby Bridges Hall." Norman Rockwell Museum. February 20, 2019. https://youtu.be/BvnxYDZ4ymY.

Herrera, Kio. "Ruby Bridges." *Time for Kids*. May 25, 2018. https://www.timeforkids.com/g56/ruby-bridges-2/.

"History—Ruby Bridges: Honorary Deputy." U.S. Marshals Service. https://www.usmarshals.gov/history/bridges/.

KEKLA MAGOON writes novels and nonfiction for young readers, including *The Highest Tribute: Thurgood Marshall's Life, Leadership, and Legacy*; *Today the World Is Watching You: The Little Rock Nine and the Fight for School Integration 1957-58*; *The Season of Styx Malone* and *The Rock and the River*. She has received the *Boston Globe-Horn Book* Award, an NAACP Image Award, the John Steptoe New Talent Award and three Coretta Scott King Honors, and has been longlisted for the National Book Award. Kekla conducts school and library visits nationwide. She holds a BA from Northwestern University and an MFA in writing from Vermont College of Fine Arts, where she now serves on faculty.

Photo credit: Alice Dodge

You can visit Kekla Magoon online at
keklamagoon.com
or follow her on Twitter
@keklamagoon

GILLIAN FLINT has worked as a professional illustrator since earning an animation and illustration degree in 2003. Her work has since been published in the UK, USA and Australia. In her spare time, Gillian enjoys reading, spending time with her family and puttering about in the garden on sunny days. She lives in the northwest of England.

You can visit Gillian Flint online at
gillianflint.com
or follow her on Twitter
@GillianFlint
and on Instagram
@gillianflint_illustration

CHELSEA CLINTON is the author of the #1 *New York Times* bestseller *She Persisted: 13 American Women Who Changed the World*; *She Persisted Around the World: 13 Women Who Changed History*; *She Persisted in Sports: American Olympians Who Changed the Game*; *Don't Let Them Disappear: 12 Endangered Species Across the Globe*; *It's Your World: Get Informed, Get Inspired & Get Going!*; *Start Now!: You Can Make a Difference*; with Hillary Clinton, *Grandma's Gardens* and *Gutsy Women*; and, with Devi Sridhar, *Governing Global Health: Who Runs the World and Why?* She is also the Vice Chair of the Clinton Foundation, where she works on many initiatives, including those that help empower the next generation of leaders. She lives in New York City with her husband, Marc, their children and their dog, Soren.

Courtesy of the author

You can follow Chelsea Clinton on Twitter
@ChelseaClinton
or on Facebook at
facebook.com/chelseaclinton

ALEXANDRA BOIGER has illustrated nearly twenty picture books, including the She Persisted books by Chelsea Clinton; the popular Tallulah series by Marilyn Singer; and the Max and Marla books, which she also wrote. Originally from Munich, Germany, she now lives outside of San Francisco, California, with her husband, Andrea, daughter, Vanessa, and two cats, Luiso and Winter.

Photo credit: *Vanessa Blasich*

You can visit Alexandra Boiger online at
alexandraboiger.com
on follow her on Instagram
@alexandra_boiger

Don't miss the rest of the books in the

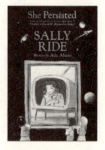
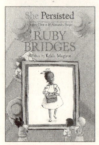

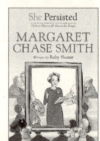

She Persisted series!

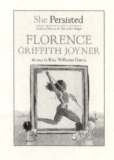
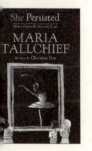

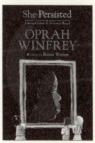